W9-BIJ-578

FREAKY TRUE SCIENCE

MORE FREAKY STORIES ABOUT OUR BODIES

BY KRISTEN RAJCZAK NELSON

Gareth Stevens
PUBLISHING

Please visit our website, www.garethstevens.com. For a free color catalog of all our high-quality books, call toll free 1-800-542-2595 or fax 1-877-542-2596.

Library of Congress Cataloging-in-Publication Data

Names: Rajczak Nelson, Kristen, author.
Title: More freaky stories about our bodies / Kristen Rajczak Nelson.
Description: New York : Gareth Stevens Publishing, [2020] | Series: Freaky true science | Includes index.
Identifiers: LCCN 2019000247| ISBN 9781538240663 (paperback) | ISBN 9781538240687 (library bound) | ISBN 9781538240670 (6 pack)
Subjects: LCSH: Medicine–Miscellanea–Juvenile literature. | Human body–Miscellanea–Juvenile literature. | Medical innovations–Juvenile literature.
Classification: LCC R706 .R36 2020 | DDC 612–dc23
LC record available at https://lccn.loc.gov/2019000247

First Edition

Published in 2020 by
Gareth Stevens Publishing
111 East 14th Street, Suite 349
New York, NY 10003

Copyright © 2020 Gareth Stevens Publishing

Designer: Sarah Liddell
Editor: Therese Shea

Photo credits: Cover, p. 1 (main) CLIPAREA | Custom media/Shutterstock.com; cover, p. 1 (leg and arm used throughout book) Morphart Creation/Shutterstock.com; background used throughout Graphic design/Shutterstock.com; hand used throughout Helena Ohman/Shutterstock.com; paper texture used throughout Alex Gontar/Shutterstock.com; p. 5 Stegerphoto/Photolibrary/Getty Images; p. 7 Dave Doe/Shutterstock.com; p. 9 (anatomy) Nerthuz/Shutterstock.com; p. 9 (organ drawings) Macrovector/Shutterstock.com; p. 11 Casa nayafana/Shutterstock.com; p. 13 BSIP/Contributor/Universal Images Group/Getty Images; p. 15 Tonhom1009/Shutterstock.com; p. 17 Quinn Rooney/Staff/Getty Images Sport/Getty Images; p. 19 Steve Jennings/Stringer/Getty Images Entertainment/Getty Images; p. 20 tab62/Shutterstock.com; p. 21 Fer Gregory/Shutterstock.com; p. 23 gosphotodesign/Shutterstock.com; p. 25 (scabies) Chuck Wagner/Shutterstock.com; p. 25 (scabies mite) molekuul_be/Shutterstock.com; p. 27 Kidsasarin bounrom/Shutterstock.com; p. 29 BSIP/UIG/Universal Images Group/Getty Images.

Printed in the United States of America

CPSIA compliance information: Batch #CS19GS: For further information contact Gareth Stevens, New York, New York at 1-800-542-2595.

CONTENTS

Words in the glossary appear in **bold** type
the first time they are used in the text.

EYE-OPENING!

Every year, doctors and scientists learn more about the human body. They can clone, or copy exactly, cells from your body. They can build usable arms and legs for people who have lost them. They can even grow organs in a lab. Some of these discoveries might freak you out!

What might be even freakier is finding out that something you believed about your body isn't exactly true. For example, did you know your eyes don't actually see? Your eyes are the organs that take in the information that allows for sight. However, it's your brain that does the seeing.

FREAKY FACTS!

Light passes through parts of the eye called the cornea, the pupil, and the lens. When it gets to the retina, special cells make the light into electrical signals that are sent to the brain.

From incredible feats of strength and endurance to the uncontrollable growth of body cells, what can happen to and in the human body is pretty amazing—and pretty freaky!

BLIND NO MORE?

There's more than one kind of blindness. Some people who are blind truly don't see anything. Others might have lost their sight over time and still see shadows, blurriness, or just not enough to experience the world like someone with full sight. A company now makes a special headset that goes over the eyes and uses a high-tech camera to allow someone who has some blindness to see words in a book or a sign down the street!

A TAIL TO TELL

Every person on Earth had a tail at one time—really! When babies are growing in their mothers' bodies, they have a tail for a short time. For almost everyone, it disappears before some women even know they're pregnant. But in some rare cases, babies are born with a tail. It can appear at the very base of their spine or even coming out of one side of their bottom. Seeing this can really freak parents out. So, most parents have these removed when the child is very young.

Babies have gills, too—sort of. They have lines on their necks as they grow inside their mothers that look a lot like gills. Scientists think they connect us to fish ancestors!

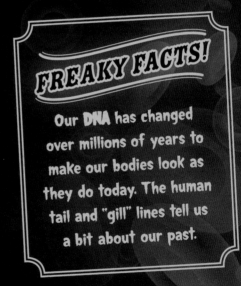

FREAKY FACTS!

Our DNA has changed over millions of years to make our bodies look as they do today. The human tail and "gill" lines tell us a bit about our past.

BORN TO WALK?

Imagine your mom tells you she is having a baby, but you don't meet your sister or brother until almost 2 years later! For a human baby to be able to walk soon after being born, a woman would have to carry it for 21 months instead of the usual 9 months. That wouldn't be healthy for the mother, though. It would take too much of her energy. The mother would die if she carried a baby that long.

HUMAN BABIES ARE QUITE HELPLESS, UNLIKE MANY OTHER MAMMALS THAT CAN WALK SOON AFTER BIRTH!

LIVING WITHOUT ORGANS

Could someone live without a brain? What about a heart? While these two organs are impossible to live without, there are other organs—or parts of organs—you *could* live without. You might need some special medical treatment, though.

You were most likely born with two lungs and two kidneys. You could survive with only one of each! In fact, once a person has a lung removed, the other lung expands to make up for it. The person might need

FREAKY FACTS!

When someone has their stomach taken out, they can still eat. They need to be careful of getting enough **nutrition**.

to exercise a little easier for the rest of their life, though. People who have a kidney removed live long, normal lives.

Perhaps most surprisingly, some people live without a stomach. They might have it removed if they have stomach **cancer**.

ORGANS YOU CAN LIVE WITHOUT

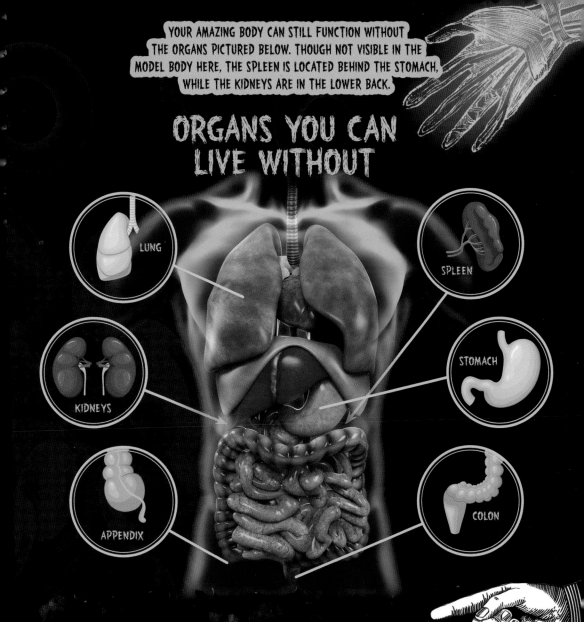

LUNG

SPLEEN

KIDNEYS

STOMACH

APPENDIX

COLON

DIALYSIS CLEANS BLOOD

Your kidneys remove waste and extra fluid from your blood.
When you only have one kidney, that job can still be done. However,
some people don't have any working kidneys. These people regularly
go through the process of dialysis, either at home or by going to
a hospital or doctor's office. Dialysis does the job of filtering the
blood, often by drawing the blood into a tube called a dialyzer,
which is filled with hollow fibers.

9

GROWTHS

Do you have a mole anywhere on your body? Or have you gotten a wart on your foot? These are tumors! Tumors are any abnormal growths on your body. Sometimes they have to do with cancer, but not always. Benign, or noncancerous, tumors grow slowly in one place.

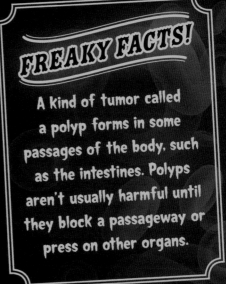

FREAKY FACTS!

A kind of tumor called a polyp forms in some passages of the body, such as the intestines. Polyps aren't usually harmful until they block a passageway or press on other organs.

In 2018, a woman in Connecticut underwent surgery for a noncancerous tumor so large it was life-threatening. It took about 5 hours to remove the 132-pound (60 kg) tumor, which started on the woman's left **ovary**. Tumors starting in this part of the body are among the largest that can occur. An ovarian tumor over 300 pounds (136 kg) has been recorded! These tumors can stretch a woman's stomach and push on blood vessels and other organs, making them very dangerous.

MORE GROWTHS

Cysts are another kind of abnormal growth in or on the body. They may not have anything to do with an illness. They commonly have liquid inside them and can grow just about anywhere on the body. Doctors often remove cysts because they can get in the way of the body's function, may have bacteria or other harmful matter inside them, and may be a sign of developing cancer.

TUMORS AND CYSTS CAN SOMETIMES BE SEEN OUTSIDE THE BODY, BUT OFTEN DOCTORS NEED TO LOOK INSIDE TO FIND THEM.

WALKING MIRACLE

In September 2018, researchers at the University of Louisville in Kentucky reported that at least five people who thought they'd never walk again due to **paralysis** did just that! A device placed in their bodies near the spinal cord provided electrical **stimulation** to their spines. This and other special physical training helped them relearn how to walk.

Why is this so freaky? The medical team that created this treatment seems to have found a route around a basic way the human body works: the spinal cord and the brain communicate to enable movement. Their results show training the spinal cord to work with the body's muscles *without* the brain is a possibility for some people with paralysis!

FREAKY FACTS!

In most of the body, new cells grow to help heal cuts, bruises, and even broken bones. However, some cells found in the central nervous system—made up of the brain and spinal cord—cannot divide and create new cells to aid the healing process.

WHEELCHAIR-BOUND

In 1995, the actor Christopher Reeve was paralyzed after breaking his neck during a riding accident. Until his death 9 years later, Reeve could only get around using a wheelchair. However, he believed that he would walk again one day. In 2000, he had begun receiving electrical stimulation to his muscles, which sometimes allowed him to feel parts of his body again. His medical team was ahead of its time.

THIS MAN IS HAVING HIS BRAIN ACTIVITY MEASURED. HE IS TAKING PART IN A COMPETITION IN WHICH ATHLETES WITH PARALYSIS USE BRAIN SIGNALS TO STEER CYCLISTS IN A VIRTUAL RACE.

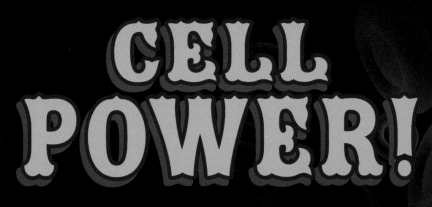

CELL POWER!

There's a medical treatment that could help people with illnesses as different as diabetes, Parkinson's disease, and heart disease. Even wilder, the basic parts needed for this treatment are found in every person on Earth: stem cells.

Stem cells are the starting point for all cells in the body. They carry instructions to become specialized cells such as blood cells, muscle cells, or nerve cells. Scientists believe they can find ways to tell a stem cell what kind of cell to become. Right now, they only know what signals to give a stem cell to create some

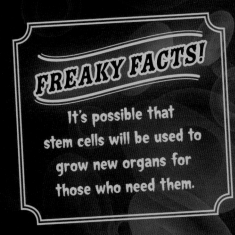

FREAKY FACTS!

It's possible that stem cells will be used to grow new organs for those who need them.

kinds of cells, though. And if the signals aren't exactly correct or are given in the wrong order, the stem cell produces a different kind of cell than a scientist wants.

STEM CELLS HAVE GIVEN PEOPLE SUFFERING FROM DISEASES HOPE FOR A CURE, BUT IT WILL TAKE TIME TO DEVELOP TREATMENTS.

FINDING STEM CELLS TO TEST

All adults have stem cells in their bodies, but they're harder for scientists to collect. They also may not live long outside the body. Stem cells for research are easier to gather from human embryos, which can be made in a lab using male and female cells. However, some people believe embryos are living human beings and they shouldn't be created in labs for scientific research.

PUSHED TO THE LIMITS

In 2006, Tom Boyle Jr. saw a young man riding a bike get hit by a car and become trapped under it. Boyle lifted the front end of the car so the victim could be pulled out. In total, the car probably weighed about 3,000 pounds (1,360 kg). It was a freaky show of strength!

However, research shows that under extreme stress, our bodies can lift much more weight than they would under normal circumstances. Even more helpful to Boyle, the body's fear response

FREAKY FACTS!

When you exercise, you create tiny tears in your muscles. Your body repairs these, and that's how your muscles grow and get stronger!

may make the body unable to feel the pain it's actually in. When he got home after the rescue, Boyle realized he had clenched his teeth so tightly while lifting the car that he broke eight teeth!

IN 2018, HAFTHOR JULIUS BJORNSSON WON THE TITLE OF WORLD'S STRONGEST MAN. HE PULLED A BUS IN ONE OF THE EVENTS! HE'S ALSO KNOWN AS THE MOUNTAIN ON THE TV SHOW *GAME OF THRONES*.

WORLD'S STRONGEST

Think about how much you weigh. Do you think you can lift twice that? With the right training and a little talent, it's possible! There are some people who have reached a freakish level of strength through training. At the World's Strongest Man event, competitors lift heavy stones, pull vehicles, and do other incredible feats. They're measured against one another by how much weight they lift, the number of repetitions they do, or how fast they finish events.

Dean Karnazes might be the ultimate example of how far a person can push their body. Known as the "Ultramarathon Man," Karnazes has run more than 100,000 miles (160,934 km) since his 30th birthday in August 1992. He ran the first marathon at the South Pole in 2002, a distance of 26.2 miles (42.2 km). In 2006, he ran 50 marathons in 50 days in all 50 states!

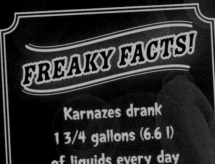

FREAKY FACTS!

Karnazes drank 1 3/4 gallons (6.6 l) of liquids every day of his 50 days of marathons. Researchers concluded that some days he could have used even more!

Karnazes may be considered a freak of nature. Though he logs thousands of training miles, he hasn't gotten injured like many long-distance runners do—except for losing a few toenails. His running form and biology have been studied, and he just might be perfectly built to run as he does!

KARNAZES RAN WITHOUT STOPPING TO EAT OR SLEEP FROM OCTOBER 12 TO OCTOBER 15, 2005. HE COVERED 350 MILES (563 KM) IN NORTHERN CALIFORNIA IN 80 HOURS AND 44 MINUTES!

INCREDIBLE KARNAZES

Before Karnazes ran his 50/50/50, no one had ever studied the effects of that kind of effort on the body. So, Karnazes gave urine and blood every 3 days during the event to a team who looked at how his body was handling the running. They found that his body was adapting to the stress. But, they also found that he was already specially adapted to the effort because of the many years he'd been running such long distances.

It's normal to want to stay up late to watch a movie with your friends, but would you ever try to stay up for days—or even a week? In 1963, two teenage boys wanted to find out how long the human body could stay awake and how the lack of sleep would affect the body. One of the boys, Randy Gardner, was awake for 11 days and 25 minutes straight, a world record.

Gardner did this by choice. However, some people stay awake and don't want to! An uncommon disease called fatal familial insomnia may keep someone awake for weeks. After a time, the person will lose weight and lose control of their muscles. It finally results in death, which scientists blame on brain damage caused by the disease.

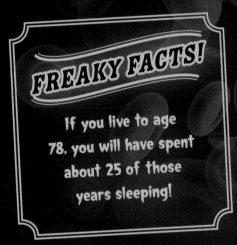

FREAKY FACTS!

If you live to age 78, you will have spent about 25 of those years sleeping!

WHAT HAPPENS WHILE YOU SLEEP?

When you don't get enough sleep, you might feel tired, sluggish, and even extra hungry. Scientists have been studying for years why people need to sleep. However, they don't have a definite answer yet. One **theory** says sleep helps our bodies repair themselves. Studies show that muscle growth and healing occur during sleep. Another theory suggests the brain changes during sleep, and this allows us to learn and do tasks better.

NOT SLEEPING ENOUGH CAN REALLY HARM YOUR HEALTH. IT'S BEEN CONNECTED TO HEART PROBLEMS, BEING OVERWEIGHT, AND THE CONDITION DIABETES.

FEEL NO PAIN

When Ashlyn Blocker was a baby, she had a scratch across her cornea, the clear layer across the front of the eye. Her eye was swollen and bloodshot—but Ashlyn was smiling and happy as the doctor looked her over. Soon after, Ashlyn was discovered to have an uncommon medical condition called congenital insensitivity to pain with anhidrosis (CIPA), which means she's unable to feel pain or temperature and cannot cool her body by sweating (anhidrosis).

By the time Ashlyn was 5 years old, she had chewed her lips until they bled as she slept at night. She got severe burns on her hands. Injuries like these are common for the very few people around the world with CIPA, especially when they are children.

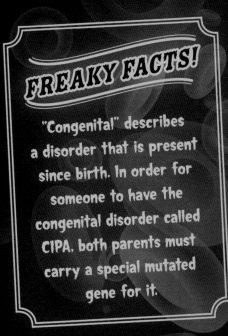

FREAKY FACTS!

"Congenital" describes a disorder that is present since birth. In order for someone to have the congenital disorder called CIPA, both parents must carry a special mutated gene for it.

BY TAKING SPECIAL CARE IN THEIR SURROUNDINGS AND AVOIDING DANGERS, PEOPLE WITH CIPA CAN LIVE TO A HEALTHY ADULTHOOD.

BE CAREFUL!

Doctors who study the small population of people with the disorder known as CIPA have found that those who have it can feel textures, hunger, and pressure, such as when they get a hug. That means CIPA only affects the parts of the nervous system that send feelings of heat, cold, and pain to the brain. Currently, there is no treatment or cure for this condition.

GETTING UNDER YOUR SKIN

You're never really alone since there are trillions of bacteria living on and in you. But most of these bacteria don't bother you. Some even help you. Certain kinds of bugs, however, are definitely going to be a bother—and their presence is likely to freak you out!

Human scabies mites are parasites that use animals, including humans, as their hosts. Adult female mites burrow into the skin to lay eggs. Then, the larvae come out of the eggs and crawl onto the surface of the skin.

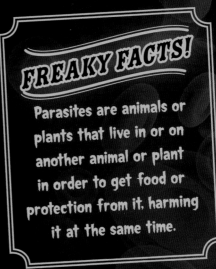

FREAKY FACTS!

Parasites are animals or plants that live in or on another animal or plant in order to get food or protection from it, harming it at the same time.

Most people who have a scabies **infestation** won't know for about a month. Then, raised red bumps and itchy patches of skin appear, often between the fingers or toes, or in the bend of a knee or elbow.

SCABIES

SCABIES MITE

CRUSTED SCABIES

Older people and those who can't fight off illness easily can get an even worse scabies infestation called crusted or Norwegian scabies. Instead of a few scabies mites making some red, itchy bumps, many scabies mites and their eggs form thick crusts of skin. Crusted scabies can be passed from person to person easily, so someone who has this kind of scabies infestation needs to be treated by a doctor right away.

SCABIES MITE LIFE CYCLE

ADULT FEMALES LAY EGGS.

EGGS HATCH INTO LARVAE.

MATING OCCURS WHEN MALES ENTER THE MOLTING POUCH OF ADULT FEMALES.

LARVAE GROW INTO NYMPHS.

LARVAE AND NYMPHS ARE FOUND IN SHALLOW BURROWS CALLED MOLTING POUCHES.

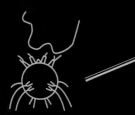

THE LIFE CYCLE OF A SCABIES MITE IS SHORT, ONLY AS LONG AS 2 MONTHS. BUT ONCE OFF THEIR HOST, THEY ONLY LIVE A FEW DAYS.

UNWELCOME GUESTS

Most people think cockroaches are gross on their own. What's grosser is finding out one has crawled into your ear while you were sleeping! To some, this might be the freakiest story of all. Roaches like to eat just about everything. The ones found in people's ears were likely looking to have an earwax snack. Over about 2 years, one South African hospital reported pulling 10 cockroaches out of patients' ears. Roaches would even be interested in chomping on the stuff that comes out of your nose! Gross!

The good news is that roaches are afraid of people. They wouldn't look for a snack in or on a person who was awake and moving around. And they certainly don't want to get stuck in a person! These are rare occurrences.

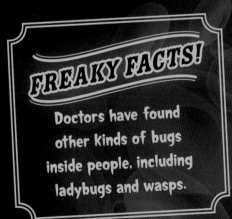

FREAKY FACTS!

Doctors have found other kinds of bugs inside people, including ladybugs and wasps.

TIDY BUGS

Most people think of roaches as being dirty. That's actually not true.
In fact, these bugs groom themselves! So, just having one on you
won't make you sick. However, bacteria in their bodies *can* make a
person sick, so it's a good idea not to crush them. If you think a bug
may have entered your ears, nose, or another body part, see a
doctor. Don't try to get it out yourself.

THE FREAKY FINISH

The freaky stories about our bodies don't stop after death. Our bodies change after death in weird ways. However, we can slow these changes with chemicals through a process called embalming. Families embalm their dead so that the body can be viewed by others days later or moved to a different place before burial.

There are many more freaky stories about the human body not in this book. For example, fibromyalgia is a condition in which people feel pain all over their body. Doctors don't know a cause yet. Some people with brain damage suddenly

FREAKY FACTS!

Embalming isn't a new idea. Ancient Egyptians practiced a kind of embalming when they created mummies.

speak with a foreign **accent**. And Cotard's syndrome is a rare condition in which people believe they're missing organs, blood, body parts—or even that they're dead. Truly, there's a lot to learn about the freaky, fascinating human body!

SOME SCIENTISTS THINK TREATING THE BRAIN WITH MAGNETIC WAVES MAY HELP RELIEVE PEOPLE'S FIBROMYALGIA PAIN. SOMETIMES, TREATMENTS CAN SEEM STRANGER THAN THE MEDICAL CONDITION ITSELF!

RELAXING MASSAGE

Massages aren't just for the living—it's also a part of embalming. Massage is a way of rubbing or pressing on a person's body to make it relax. This is helpful for aches and pains in the living, but it also helps relieve rigor mortis, or the stiffness of the body that occurs after someone dies. Rigor mortis, which is Latin for "stiffness of death," occurs because of chemical changes in the body after death.

GLOSSARY

accent: a way of saying words that occurs among the people in a region or country

cancer: a disease caused by the uncontrolled growth of cells in the body

DNA: part of the body that carries genetic information, which gives the instructions for life

filter: to collect bits from a liquid passing through

infestation: the presence of living things in large numbers that can cause harm

nutrition: things that living things need to grow and stay alive

ovary: one of two organs in women that make eggs for human reproduction

paralysis: the state of being unable to move

stimulation: the act of encouraging something to make it develop or make it more active

theory: a general idea that explains something

urine: a yellow liquid containing water and waste products that flows out of an animal's body

FOR MORE INFORMATION

BOOKS

Braun, Eric. *Awesome, Disgusting, Unusual Facts About the Human Body.* Mankato, MN: Black Rabbit Books, 2019.

Hutmacher, Kimberly. *Your Nose Never Stops Growing And Other Cool Human Body Facts.* North Mankato, MN: Capstone Press, 2019.

Rhatigan, Joe. *50 Wacky Things Humans Do: Weird and Amazing Facts About Our Bodies!* Minneapolis, MN: Walter Foster Jr., 2019.

WEBSITES

How the Body Works
kidshealth.org/kid/htbw/
Discover more about how the human body works here.

Human Biology
kidsbiology.com/human-biology/
Review all the human body systems on this website for kids.

INDEX